# DISASTER!
# WEATHER

## Jen Green

Belitha Press

## LOOK FOR THE HURRICANE

Look for the hurricane in boxes like this.
Here you will find extra facts, stories and other
interesting information about weather disasters.

Produced by
Monkey Puzzle Media Ltd,
Gissing's Farm, Fressingfield,
Suffolk IP21 5SH, UK

First published in the UK in 2002 by
Belitha Press Limited, A member of **Chrysalis** Books plc
64 Brewery Road, London N7 9NT

Designer: Victoria Webb
Editor: Kate Phelps
Picture Research: Lynda Lines

ISBN 1 84138 412 7

British Library Cataloguing in Publication Data for this book is available from the
British Library.

Printed in Taiwan
10 9 8 7 6 5 4 3 2 1

**Acknowledgements**
We wish to thank the following individuals and organizations for their help and
assistance and for supplying material in their collections: Corbis 3 (Bettmann),
10 top (Bettmann), 15 bottom (Bettmann), 21 bottom (Reuters), 22 (Bettmann),
26 (Pat O'Hara), 27 (Sergio Dorantes); FLPA 6 (AIS), 14 top (Silvestris
Fotoservice), 14 bottom (Servicio Aero-Foto); ICRC back cover top (Sharilyn
Amy), 13 (Sharilyn Amy); NASA back cover bottom right, 28; Oxford Scientific
Films front cover (Kent Wood), back cover bottom left (Laurence Gould),
9 bottom (Laurence Gould), 16 (Warren Faidley), 17 (Kent Wood), 23 top
(Warren Faidley); Popperfoto 15 top (Jose Miguel Gomez/Reuters); Rex Features
7 top (Fidelin), 9 top, 10 bottom (Sipa), 11 top (Sipa), 12 top (Sipa), 18 (Sipa),
25 bottom (Sipa); Topham Picturepoint 1, 2, 4, 5 bottom, 11 bottom, 12 bottom
(T Maury), 19 top, 20, 21 top, 23 bottom, 24, 25 top, 29 (F Chowdhury).
Artwork by Michael Posen.

▼ *Soldiers help to clear the*
*wreckage after a flood in the*
*city of Florence, Italy in 1966.*

# CONTENTS

► *In 1900, a storm destroyed the port of Galveston, USA. Waves washed over the town and swept away this schoolhouse.*

# EXTREME WEATHER

**T**he weather on our planet, including sunshine, winds and rain, provides all the conditions needed for life to flourish. Most of the time, the weather is kind to us, but sometimes it is cruel.

Severe weather conditions include hurricanes, floods, landslides, drought and blizzards. All of these natural hazards can be killers. They can cause damage costing millions of pounds and wipe out whole neighbourhoods.

Powerful storms called hurricanes and tornadoes can cause great destruction. Heavy rain brings floods that drown whole valleys. On steep slopes in mountains, snowy avalanches and rock landslides bring disaster when they crash down.

► *Tornadoes are violent spinning winds that can be very destructive. The twisting column of air sucks up all kinds of heavy objects and lifts them high in the air.*

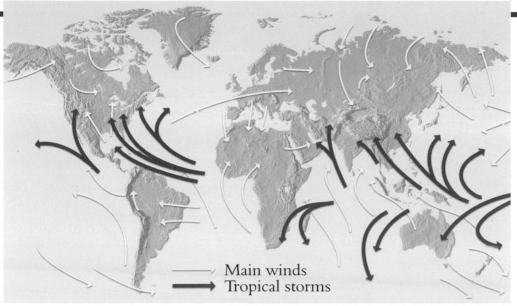

◄ *The yellow arrows on this map show the world's main winds. The winds are bent by the spin of the Earth. Tropical storms – hurricanes and cyclones – are shown by the red arrows.*

→ Main winds
➡ Tropical storms

Dry weather brings droughts, during which people can die of thirst or hunger. Winter brings the threat of icy blizzards which can kill with cold.

All the weather on our planet is caused by the air warming or cooling. Differences in temperature between air masses in different places create strong winds, which bring clear weather or stormy skies.

▲ *Hurricanes are violent storms that mainly strike in warm weather. In September 1995, the port of St Thomas in the Virgin Islands in the Caribbean was wrecked by Hurricane Marilyn.*

## THUNDERSTORMS AND LIGHTNING

Thunderstorms begin when warm, moist air rises quickly to form dark clouds. Inside the clouds, winds cause water drops and ice crystals to rub together, creating electricity. The electric charge is released when lightning flashes down to the ground.

# DEADLY HURRICANES

**H**urricanes are violent, spinning storms with winds whirling round at great speed. They begin over tropical oceans and cause great damage when they reach land.

Most hurricanes strike in summer. In Australia, summer comes at Christmas. In 1974, a hurricane wrecked the coastal town of Darwin in northern Australia on Christmas Day.

In Australia, hurricanes are called cyclones. On Christmas Eve, Australian weather experts said that a violent storm called Cyclone Tracy was brewing to the north. In Darwin, people were too busy preparing for Christmas to take much notice. The experts thought the storm would miss Australia and stay out to sea. During the night, Cyclone Tracy swooped south towards Darwin. The full force of the storm struck the town at 4 am. Trees were uprooted and roofs were torn off houses.

◄ *Cyclone Tracy was one of the worst hurricanes ever to hit Australia. It destroyed 8000 homes in Darwin. Fifty people died, but the figure would have been much higher if the cyclone had struck during the day.*

*In September 1989, Hurricane Hugo struck the Caribbean island of Guadaloupe, causing bad flooding.*

## SAVED BY HURRICANES

In 1274 and 1281, hurricanes prevented the invasion of Japan by Chinese emperor Kublai Khan. On each occasion, the Chinese fleet was wrecked before it could land. The Japanese believed that the gods had saved them. They called the hurricanes kamikaze, which means 'divine winds'.

People were woken up by howling winds and crashing glass and metal. They looked out to see planks of wood and even cars flying down the street. The cyclone raged for four hours but died down by daybreak. People came out to find that 90 per cent of the town had been destroyed.

*Hurricanes are huge swirling storms that may be hundreds of kilometres across. From above, they look like giant catherine wheels made of spinning clouds. The winds inside some hurricanes reach speeds of 300 km/h.*

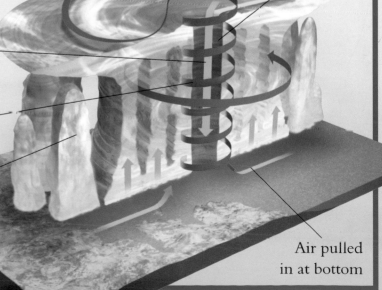

Eye of hurricane

Air sinks down in centre of eye

Air is pulled up around centre of hurricane and swirls outwards

Strong winds spin clouds around eye of hurricane

Air pulled in at bottom

# TERRIFYING TORNADOES

A tornado is a whirling column of air that forms under a thundercloud. These spinning storms are also called twisters. They are much smaller than hurricanes, but can be even more deadly.

Tornadoes can strike anywhere, but they are most common in central USA in an area called Tornado Alley. Sometimes a whole group, or swarm, of tornadoes strikes at once. On 3-4 April 1974, a swarm of 148 tornadoes roared across central USA.

The town of Xenia, Ohio, lay in the heart of the danger zone. A powerful twister struck Xenia High School at 4.30 pm. Luckily, most pupils had gone home. One girl, Ruth Venuti, saw the tell-tale funnel of dark smoke approaching. She rushed back to the school hall to warn students who were rehearsing a play.

## EYE OF THE STORM

The powerful winds in a tornado spin around a calm, central area called the eye. Only a few people have stood in the eye of the storm and lived to tell the tale. They describe looking up past walls of dark, rotating clouds to catch a glimpse of clear sky beyond.

▶ *The winds inside a tornado whirl round at high speed, creating a tall funnel. The spinning column picks up dirt and wreckage as it moves along.*

Air sinking down

Eye

Air sucked in at bottom spirals upwards

On 21-22 November 1992, a swarm of tornadoes hit southern USA. This district of Houston, Texas, was flattened by one of the tornadoes. At least 26 people were killed by the swarm.

In coastal areas, powerful tornadoes toss boats around like toys. On the Caribbean island of Bermuda, this boat was blown up the beach and hurled into a tree.

The children ran for cover as the storm struck. They ducked low as flying earth, shattered glass and splinters of wood swept over their heads. When the storm passed, they found that the whole top floor of the school had been blown off. The school bus lay smashed on the stage where they had been standing. Ruth's warning had come not a moment too soon.

# SURGING SEAS

**H**urricanes can whip up towering seas that threaten coastal regions. High tides called storm surges can sweep in to flood villages and towns on low-lying coasts.

Storm surges have caused terrible floods in Bangladesh in southern Asia. This low-lying country lies by the Indian Ocean. It includes many islands that rise only a few metres above the sea.

In April 1991, thousands of people on the islands were threatened when a powerful hurricane blew in from the ocean. In the evening, villagers noticed huge red storm clouds gathering out to sea.

On the island of Maiskhal, one young teacher was giving a lesson in his hut when the storm broke. He didn't take much notice until a violent wind blew the roof off. As the winds grew stronger, towering waves crashed over the islands. People hugged each other as the water smashed on to their huts.

*▲ In 1900, the port of Galveston in southern USA, shown here, was destroyed by a hurricane and storm surge. The town had been built on a low island off the coast. Around 6000 people died when waves washed over the island. It was one of the worst disasters in US history.*

*▶ Bangladesh has been hit by flooding many times. In 1998, floods killed at least 800 people and made millions homeless. People climbed on to the roofs of their houses to escape the rising tide.*

The hurricane battered Bangladesh for seven hours. Many islands were completely awash. People, animals and homes were swept away in the stormy waters. 'I was terrified, so I sang lullabies,' said Moni, a ten-year-old boy.

▲ *Over 138 000 people died in the floods after the hurricane struck Bangladesh in April 1991. The floodwaters wrecked millions of homes.*

## THE GREAT FLOOD

The Bible's Old Testament tells of a flood that struck western Asia after rain fell for 40 days and nights without stopping. Water covered the whole Earth, and almost everyone drowned. Only Noah and his family were saved because God warned them to build a boat called an ark. Recently, scientists have found traces of a great flood that struck the region about 4000 years ago. It may have inspired the Bible story.

# RAGING RIVERS

**A**ll over the world, people live by rivers because the soil is fertile and good for farming. But every now and then, most rivers burst their banks and flood the surrounding land.

River levels often rise after heavy rain has fallen or when the snow melts in springtime. In the summer of 1993, terrible floods struck the Midwest in central USA after months of heavy rain.

Two great rivers, the Mississippi and the Missouri, rose higher and higher and then burst their banks. High walls called levees had been built along the rivers to prevent flooding, but they failed to keep the rising waters at bay.

▲ *During the floods of 1993, farmers and army troops stacked millions of sandbags along the rivers, but failed to control the rising water.*
*'It's like watching a disaster movie,' one worker said.*

◄ *People work together to stack sandbags to protect shops and businesses in towns threatened by the floods of 1993.*

As the floods spread over the countryside, fields became lakes and streams gushed through towns. People grabbed a few precious possessions and dashed to the safety of high ground.

The floods eventually covered 40 000 sq km of land and caused millions of pounds of damage. The US president declared the region a disaster zone. 'Hurricanes are devastating, but at least they're over quickly,' said a rescue worker. 'This is cruel. The water just sits around.'

## DEADLY RIVERS OF CHINA

In China, huge numbers of people live in the valleys of two mighty rivers, the Yangtze and the Yellow River. But both rivers have a bad history of flooding. In 1938, thousands of people died when the Yangtze burst its banks. The river has flooded many times since.

▼ *During floods in China in 1998, people clung to floating objects to save themselves from drowning. The Yellow River is known as 'China's sorrow' because it has flooded so often. In 1938, around 90 000 people died in a terrible flood.*

# AVALANCHES AND LANDSLIDES

▲ *Snow cascades down a mountain during an avalanche in the Alps in Switzerland.*

**A**valanches and landslides strike when a mass of loose snow, ice or earth breaks off a mountain and rushes downhill. The disaster may be triggered by heavy rain or snowfall or by hot sun melting the ice.

On 10 January 1962, a deadly avalanche began high in the Andes Mountains in South America. A day of sunshine had melted the ice on a high peak called Huascarán. At sunset, a large chunk of ice broke off the mountain. It hurtled downhill, gathering rock and snow.

Several villages and the town of Ranrahirca lay on the slopes below the mountain. People heard a roaring sound and looked up. They saw what looked like a golden cloud near the summit. But the 'cloud' was flying downhill.

◀ *The Peruvian town of Ranrahirca and four villages were wiped out by the avalanche that swept down from Mount Huascarán in 1962.*

*◄ In 1999, landslides and flash floods engulfed the town of La Guaira and the area around it in Venezuela, South America. At least 10 000 people were killed and 200 000 more were made homeless.*

With a mighty roar, a tide of snow, ice and mud swept into the highest village. Buildings crumbled like dolls' houses. The avalanche then struck Ranrahirca in the valley below.

When the avalanche finally stopped, a tide of rock and mud 18m deep filled the green valley. Around 3500 people died in the disaster. 'When I came to my senses, I saw only a waste of mud and ice,' one survivor said.

*▼ The avalanche on Mount Huascarán in 1962 made thousands of people homeless. These survivors are waiting to receive shelter and food.*

## 🌀 DAM BURST

In 1963, the Vaiont Dam high in the Italian Alps burst after a landslide began on a nearby mountain. The landslide filled the lake behind the dam with earth. This sent a wall of water surging over the dam and down into the valley. Around 4000 people died in the villages below.

15

# THUNDERSTORMS, HAIL AND LIGHTNING

**A**bout 45 000 thunderstorms strike around the world each day. That's an average of 30 every minute! When a storm breaks, lightning flashes and thunder rolls. Torrents of rain, sleet or hail lash down.

In 1959, American pilot William Rankin was caught in a mid-air thunderstorm. He had to bale out of his plane at a height of 14 000 m when his engine developed a fault. Rankin's parachute opened safely, but he was whirled around inside the storm cloud instead of dropping gently to the ground.

'I was buffeted in all directions – up, down, sideways, over and over,' Rankin reported. 'I was stretched, slammed and pounded…and shot up like a shell from a cannon.'

## HOW HAILSTONES FORM

Hailstones are balls of ice that form when winds toss ice crystals up and down inside thunderclouds. Each time the crystal rises, a new layer of ice forms around it. Finally, the hailstone gets so heavy it drops to the ground.

▲ *This large hailstone is small compared to the whopper stone that fell in a farmyard in Kansas, USA, in 1970. The huge stone was the size of a melon and weighed 0.75 kg. It was the largest ever recorded in the USA.*

It was raining so heavily inside the cloud Rankin thought he would drown in mid-air. He was so frightened he shut his eyes for most of the time. Finally, he glimpsed green fields coming up towards him and crash-landed in a tree.

In all the terrified pilot spent 40 minutes in the heart of a thunderstorm before finally landing. He was covered with cuts and bruises but otherwise unhurt and was soon flying again.

▲ *Lightning streaks down from a thundercloud during a violent storm in Tucson, USA. The electric charges that build up inside the dark clouds are caused by frozen water droplets crashing together.*

# IN THE GRIP OF DROUGHT

**D**roughts are long periods of dry weather which bring great hardship and even starvation. They are the biggest killers of all weather hazards in the world.

During a bad drought, lakes dry up and rivers dwindle to muddy trickles. Crops wither and die, then farm animals starve. Water becomes scarce and there is nothing for people to eat.

Drought is a major problem in Africa. In 1963-73, a terrible drought hit West Africa. Crops died and fields turned to dust. The Sahara Desert expanded and spread southwards. The town of Timbuktu in Mali once lay at the heart of fertile farmland. Now it is surrounded by desert sands.

▼ *Victims of the drought in Somalia in 1992 receive food in a refugee camp. Aid workers from Western countries help by providing basic foods such as cornmeal, beans and milk.*

## DUST BOWL DANGER

In the 1930s, a decade of drought hit the American Midwest. Crops died, and powerful winds blew away the dusty soil. The Midwest became a 'dust bowl'. Farming families had to leave or face starvation. The Midwest took years to recover from the terrible drought.

▲ *Midwestern farming families pray for rain during the Dust Bowl drought of the 1930s.*

In 1991-3, drought struck again, this time in East Africa. Faced with starvation, people left their homes and fled to refugee camps to find food. Muslima, a woman from Somalia, arrived at a camp alone. She had fled with her mother and two children, but they had all died on the journey. 'I have buried all my family. Almost everyone from my village is dead. I have no more tears left,' she said.

New farming methods can help fight the problem of drought in Africa. So can digging wells and building dams to store water.

Areas regularly affected by drought

▲ *A third of all the land on Earth is hit by drought from time to time. The worst droughts happen in Africa and Asia. South America and Australia also suffer bad droughts.*

# THE LITTLE ICE AGE

▼ *This old illustration shows the frost fair on the River Thames during the icy winter of 1677.*

An Ice Age is a very long period of cold weather when ice covers much of the Earth. The last true Ice Age ended many thousands of years ago, but between 1400 and 1850, the world suffered a mini Ice Age.

During the Little Ice Age, temperatures were considerably colder than they are today. Many winters were bitterly cold, and rivers and lakes froze over for months.

## FROST FAIRS

From 1600 to the early 1800s, the River Thames in London froze over regularly. Frost fairs were held on the ice, with sideshows and hot food stalls. In 1812-13, the year of Napoleon's retreat, the ice was thick enough to support the weight of an elephant, which became a major attraction. After 1813, the weather grew warmer and the Thames has never frozen since.

The winter of 1812-13 was particularly savage. It changed the course of history by destroying the army of French emperor, Napoleon Bonaparte. At the time, France was at war with Russia. In autumn 1812, Napoleon's army had fought its way across Russia to enter the capital, Moscow. The retreating Russians set fire to the city.

▲ *During the winter of 1812-13, retreating French troops survived on an uncooked 'stew' of snow and horsemeat. Of the 450 000 soldiers that set out to conquer Russia, less than one in ten returned.*

Now the French troops had no food or shelter for the coming winter. Napoleon had to order his army to retreat. The French staggered back through terrible blizzards, with almost no food. Thousands died of cold and starvation.

▶ *The town of Buffalo in eastern USA is often struck by blizzards in winter. During the cold winter of 1976-77, a thick blanket of snow buried highways and vehicles. Many homes were cut off. Another major blizzard, shown here, hit in 2000-1.*

# AMAZING SURVIVORS

W eather hazards such as hurricanes and floods are major killers. Sometimes they wipe out almost everyone in the stricken area. Only a lucky few are left alive.

Along the east coast of North America, hurricanes are quite common in summer. In the 1950s and 60s, people became so casual about them they began to hold 'hurricane parties' instead of leaving the danger zone.

On 17 August 1969, two dozen people gathered for a hurricane party in luxury flats on the beach in Pass Christian, Mississippi. Hurricane Camille was due to strike the coast about 160 km to the east. Party-goers such as Mary Ann Gerlach thought they could watch the storm safely. But at the last minute, the hurricane changed course.

◀ *Hurricane Camille wrecked many holiday resorts, including this one in Bay St Louis, Mississippi. Camille killed a total of 256 people, including everyone at the hurricane party in Pass Christian except Mary Ann Gerlach.*

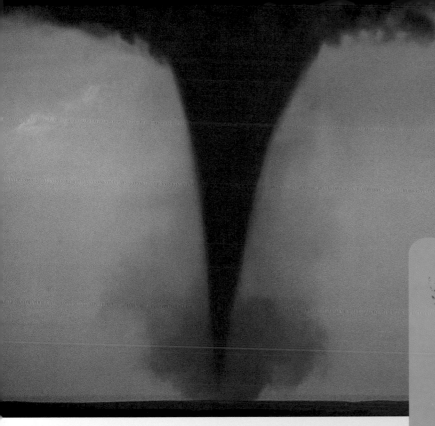

▲ *The dark funnel of a tornado sweeps through 'Tornado Alley' in southern USA.*

## STRUCK BY LIGHTNING

Park ranger Roy Sullivan from Virginia, USA, survived being struck by lightning seven times between 1942 and 1977. In 1969, lightning singed his eyebrows. In 1972 and again in 1973, it set light to his hair. In 1976, it burned his ankle and, in 1977, his chest, but Sullivan survived every strike.

As the hurricane hit Pass Christian, all the windows in the flats were broken. Towering waves from the ocean filled the building to the second floor. Mary Ann reported 'You could feel the building swaying like in a boat.' She swam out of a second-floor window. Seconds later, the whole block of flats collapsed into the waves.

Mary Ann clung to some wreckage and was swept 8 km inland. In the morning, rescuers found her in the top of a tree. The disaster changed Mary Ann's mind about hurricane parties: 'Now when there's a hurricane warning, I get out with all the rest.'

▼ *Lightning brightens the night sky above Ayers Rock (Uluru) in Australia.*

# TO THE RESCUE

**D**isasters such as tornadoes and landslides are over in a matter of minutes. Some weather hazards last for longer, but the damage they cause takes months, even years, to repair.

When severe weather strikes, the rescue services race to the stricken zone as quickly as possible. If the roads are wrecked, they often come by plane. They search for survivors among the ruins. Injured people are rushed to hospital. Other survivors are given shelter, water and food.

Later, workers start to clear the wreckage. Buildings are made safe and bridges and roads are rebuilt so people can come and go more easily. Finally the work of rebuilding begins, so survivors can return if they wish.

▼ *In 1966, the River Arno burst its banks in Florence, Italy. The city's priceless art collection was threatened. Everyone helped to carry paintings, sculptures and other treasures to high ground. Soldiers, seen here, also helped with the clean-up operation.*

# PREDICTING WEATHER HAZARDS

Hurricanes and other natural disasters can't be prevented. But if weather centres broadcast warnings, people can prepare or even leave the region if they can. Hours before Hurricane Andrew struck, local weather forecasters warned people to get ready for 'the big one'. The warning helped to reduce the number of people who died.

▶ *A forecaster working at the National Hurricane Centre in the USA keeps a close eye on a hurricane using pictures taken by a satellite.*

In August 1992, Hurricane Andrew struck southeastern USA. The army were brought in to help clean up and distribute food. 'We're approaching this like a war, except we're putting troops in to help people, not kill them,' said an officer. The army also helped to restore calm when looting (stealing) broke out.

Ordinary people from other parts of the USA sent foods, tents and other supplies to the stricken area. Some even turned up to volunteer for repair work. A forklift truck driver called Steve Rodriguez arrived, saying 'I want to help. I heard it in the news, and I couldn't bear it. I told my boss and my wife I had to go.'

▶ *Rescuers race to save the lives of victims caught in an avalanche in the Alps in February 2000.*

*Life goes on as usual despite deep snow at the visitor centre in Paradise, USA, which has received record-breaking levels of snow in some years.*

# DISASTER FACTS

### STRONGEST HURRICANE

The most powerful hurricane ever recorded was Hurricane Gilbert, which struck the Caribbean in 1988. It wrecked thousands of homes and caused millions of pounds of damage. About 300 people were killed.

### DEADLY TWISTER

The world's deadliest tornado struck Bangladesh in southern Asia in April 1989. No one knows how many people died in the disaster, but experts think it may have been as many as 1300.

### TORNADO WITNESS

In 1928, American farmer Will Keller became one of the very few people who have ever survived in the eye of a tornado. He later reported: 'The great shaggy end of the funnel hung directly overhead…There was a screaming, hissing sound coming from the funnel. I looked up and to my astonishment, I saw right up into the heart of the tornado. There was a circular opening extending straight upward…The walls of this opening were rotating clouds.'

## A TORNADO IN THE HENHOUSE

In 1977, a tornado burst on to a farm in Alabama, USA, and wrecked the henhouse. The twister plucked out the terrified chickens' feathers but did not otherwise harm the birds.

## SWEET DREAMS

In 1981, a tornado in Ancona, Italy, lifted a baby from its pram. It carried the child for a distance of 90 m before dropping it gently to the ground. The baby remained asleep during the ride.

## WORST FLOOD

The world's worst flood happened in China in October 1887. The Yellow River burst its banks and flooded the surrounding countryside. Nearly a million people died.

## SNOWIEST TOWN

A town called Paradise on Mount Ranier, Washington, USA, holds the record for the highest snowfall in one year. It received 32 m of snow between February 1971 and February 1972.

## KILLER HAILSTONES

Rain and sleet can sting, but only hailstones can hurt you. In 1986, 92 people died during a freak thunderstorm in Bangladesh. Giant hailstones the size of grapefruits rained down.

## HAILSTORM STOPS PARADE

In 1995, a violent hailstorm struck a May parade in Fort Worth, Texas, USA. People marching through the streets were hit by hailstones the size of tennis balls. The hail also smashed windows and car windscreens. Ninety people were injured by the stones and broken glass.

## ICE STORM

In January 1997, eastern Canada and northeast USA suffered the worst blizzard for decades. Freezing rain fell which soon turned to solid ice. Trees, roofs and even electricity pylons collapsed under the weight of the ice. A major power cut plunged four million people into icy darkness.

▶ *This Cuban fishing boat was thrown high on the beach by Hurricane Gilbert, which struck the Caribbean in 1988.*

# DISASTER WORDS

**Aid worker**  Someone who works for an organization that supplies food and other help to victims of disasters.

**Avalanche**  A mass of loose snow, ice and rocks that crashes downhill at high speed.

**Blizzard**  A violent snowstorm.

**Cyclone**  Another name for a hurricane.

**Drought**  A long period of dry weather during which hardly any rain falls.

**Dust Bowl**  A region of the Midwest in the United States that was struck by drought during the 1930s.

**Eye**  A region of calm air found in the centre of a hurricane or tornado.

**Frost fair**  A fair held on a frozen lake or river.

**Hail**  Balls of ice that form inside thunderclouds as winds toss ice crystals up and down.

**Humidity**  The amount of moisture in the air.

**Hurricane**  A violent tropical storm with spinning winds. Hurricanes are also known as cyclones and typhoons.

**Landslide**  A mass of loose earth and rock that slips downhill on a steep slope.

**Levee**  A wall built along a river bank to prevent flooding.

◄ *This image of a hurricane about to strike the coast of southeastern USA was taken by a satellite. The hurricane's eye can be clearly seen.*

▲ *A boy from Bangladesh tries to save his goats from the flood waters by transporting them on a raft.*

**Midwest** The north central part of the USA.

**Refugee** Someone who leaves his or her home after drought, war or another disaster.

**Storm surge** Towering waves that are whipped up by hurricanes and cause very high tides when they reach land.

**Tornado** A whirling funnel of air that stretches down from a thundercloud. Tornadoes are smaller than hurricanes, but sometimes contain even stronger winds.

**Tornado Alley** A region in central USA where tornadoes often strike.

**Tornado swarm** A group of tornadoes that all strike a region in the space of just one or two days.

**Tropical** Situated in the hot area of the Earth between the tropics and the Equator.

**Typhoon** Another name for a hurricane.

**Wind** A movement of air from one place to another.

# DISASTER PROJECTS

**S**cientists keep a close eye on the weather to try to predict weather hazards. You, too, can become a weather expert by setting up your own weather station, listening to forecasts and logging on to weather sites on the Internet.

There are now over 50 000 weather stations worldwide. They measure conditions including air temperature and moisture, wind speed and direction, and snow or rainfall. High in space, satellites track storm clouds, hurricanes and other weather systems. All of this information helps scientists to produce weather forecasts which are then broadcast on TV, radio and the Internet.

Set up your own weather station by making a wind vane and rain gauge. It would help to have a thermometer to measure air temperatures and a barometer to measure humidity (the amount of moisture in the air).

Keep a weather diary with all your measurements in a notebook or on the computer. Take temperature readings at the same time each day, for example, in the morning, at lunchtime and at night. Note down wind direction, rainfall and whether the day was bright, cloudy or rainy. Listen to the weather forecast and see if it matches your records.

Balsa wood

Modelling clay

Garden cane

Beads

Bamboo

▶ *A wind vane shows the direction the wind is blowing. You can make one with a garden cane, hollow bamboo tube and balsa wood. Ask an adult to help you cut the balsa into three pieces as shown. Cut slots and then glue the pieces together. Make a hole in the vane and push it on to the cane. Then slot the cane into the bamboo tube pushed into the ground. Beads placed as shown will help the vane spin in the wind.*

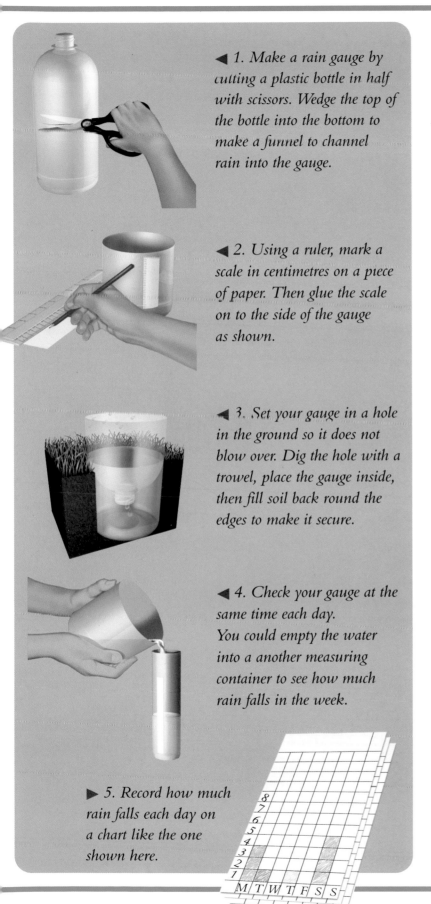

◀ 1. Make a rain gauge by cutting a plastic bottle in half with scissors. Wedge the top of the bottle into the bottom to make a funnel to channel rain into the gauge.

◀ 2. Using a ruler, mark a scale in centimetres on a piece of paper. Then glue the scale on to the side of the gauge as shown.

◀ 3. Set your gauge in a hole in the ground so it does not blow over. Dig the hole with a trowel, place the gauge inside, then fill soil back round the edges to make it secure.

◀ 4. Check your gauge at the same time each day. You could empty the water into a another measuring container to see how much rain falls in the week.

▶ 5. Record how much rain falls each day on a chart like the one shown here.

## WEATHER WATCH WEBSITES

*If you have access to the Internet, there are hundreds of websites you can call up to find out more about the weather and weather hazards.*

*Websites change from time to time, so don't worry if you can't find some of these sites. You can also search for sites featuring hurricanes, tornadoes, floods and avalanches using any search engine.*

### SEVERE WEATHER WATCH WEBSITES
*US national weather service, with weather warnings: www.crh.noaa.gov*
*UK weather service, with weather warnings: www.weather.org.uk*
*Storm watch: www.stormwarn.com*
*Global disaster watch: www.angelfire.com/on/predictions*

### HURRICANE WEBSITES
*Hurricane watch: www.hurricane.com*
*Hurricane news: www.hurricanenews.com*

### TORNADO WEBSITES
*Twister!: www.weathereye.kgan.com*
*Tornado watch: www.earthwatch.com*

### AVALANCHE WEBSITES
*Avalanche watch: www.avalanche.org*
*Avalanche warnings: www.csac.org*

# INDEX

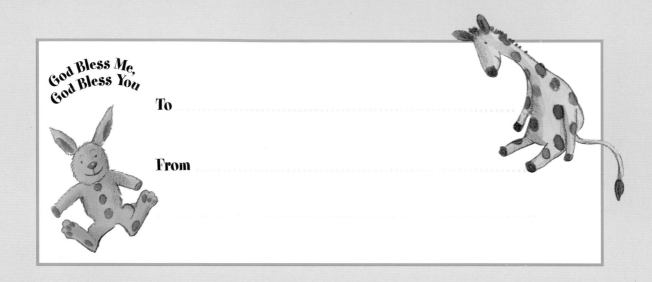

God Bless Me,
God Bless You

To ..................................................................................

From ..............................................................................

Text by Lois Rock
Illustrations copyright © 2001 John Bendall-Brunello
This edition copyright © 2001 Lion Publishing

The moral rights of the author and illustrator
have been asserted

Published by
**Lion Publishing plc**
Sandy Lane West, Oxford, England
www.lion-publishing.co.uk
ISBN 0 7459 4265 2

First edition 2001
1 3 5 7 9 10 8 6 4 2 0

A catalogue record for this book is available
from the British Library

Typeset in 24/32 Baskerville MT Schlbk
Printed and bound in Singapore

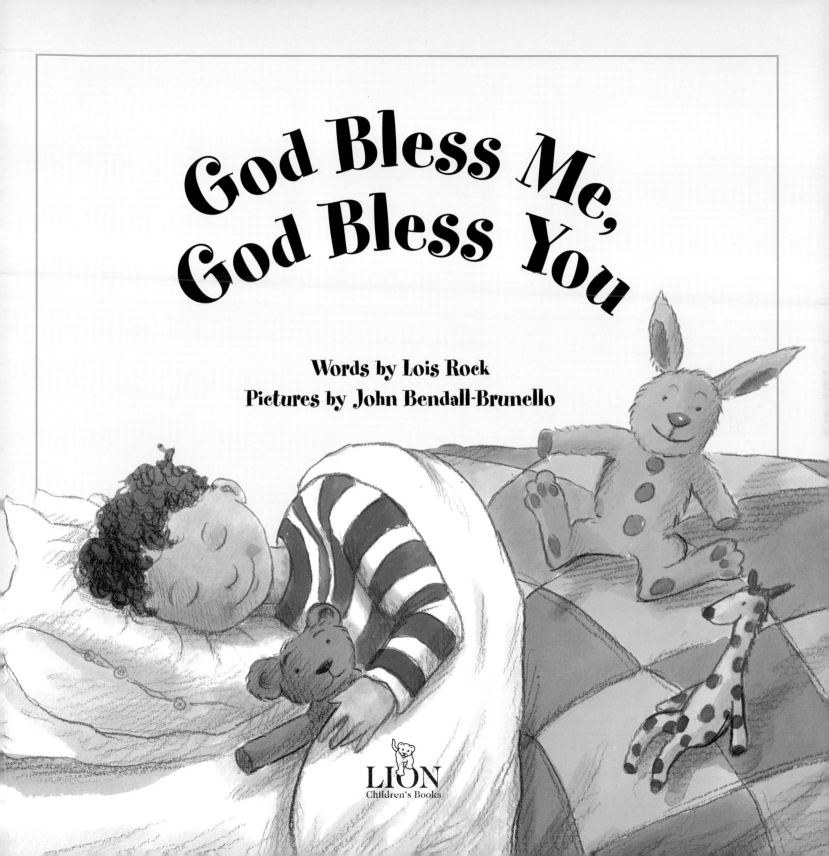

# God Bless Me, God Bless You

Words by Lois Rock

Pictures by John Bendall-Brunello

LION
Children's Books

The day is over, night is near,
There's one more thing to do –
Let's say a prayer to God above:
God bless me, God bless you.

Dear God, bless everything you made,
The daytime and the night,

The sun, the moon and all the stars
That shine with twinkling light.

God bless the hills that stand so tall,
God bless the fields so green,
God bless the seas, God bless the waves,
God bless each rippling stream.

Let flowers close their petals now
And may the night-time breeze
Blow gently through the grasses and
The whispering forest trees.

Remember, too, O Maker God,
The creatures of the day.
In cosy homes may each one sleep
The night-time hours away.

Now all the creatures of the night
Awake, and softly creep

On grey and silver woodland paths
While we are fast asleep.

Please take good care of those we love
Who help us every day,
Who bring us all the things we need
And still have time to play.

Take care of loved ones far away,
Who watch the shining moon
And think of us with sighs and smiles
And hope to see us soon.

Now, as the earth turns, other lands
Can see the sun above.
May all the peoples of the world
Find happiness and love.

Dear God, now let me say goodbye
To all that I have done.
Help me forgive the horrid things,
Remember all the fun.

May I sleep deep and dreamily
Till darkness slips away.
I'll wake up with the golden sun
All ready for the day.

Now night has come and we are tired.
There's nothing left to do,
For God is love, and God above
Will bless both me and you.